A Ticket to
Canada

Janice Hamilton

Carolrhoda Books, Inc. / Minneapolis

Photo Acknowledgments

Photos, maps, and artworks are used courtesy of: John Erste, pp. 1, 2–3, 13, 16–17, 27, 34–35, 39, 41, 42–43; Laura Westlund, pp. 4–5, 18, 21; Voscar—The Maine Photographer, pp. 6, 13 (top), 26 (far left), 26 (far right); © Robert Fried, pp. 7 (top), 8, 11 (left), 14 (right), 15 (both), 18, 20 (right), 21, 28, 44; © Tourism New Brunswick, p. 7 (bottom); © John Elk, pp. 9 (top), 22 (left), 23 (bottom), 32–33, 34, 36 (right), 38 (right), 40, 42; Tourism Saskatchewan, p. 9 (bottom); Ministry of Forests/Forestry Canada, p. 10; © Jerry Hennen, pp. 11 (right), 13 (bottom), 35; © Nunavut Tourism, pp. 12, 17 (top); © TRIP/Yona Kruch, p. 14 (left); © TRIP/Eric Smith, p. 16, 19, 32; © Lyn Hancock, pp. 17 (bottom), 22 (right), 30 (right), 36 (left), 37 (top); Winston Fraser, p. 18; © Duncan McDougall/Diarama Stock Photos, Inc., p. 19; © Steve Warble, pp. 23 (top), 33; © Excel Images, Inc./Canadian Tourism Commission, p. 23 (inset); © Yvonne McDougall/Diarama Stock Photos, Inc., p. 24 (top); © Wes Bergen/Diarama Stock Photos, Inc., pp. 24 (bottom), 31 (middle); © Marja Bergen/Diarama Stock Photos, Inc., pp. 25, 31 (top); Tourisme Québec/Jean Sylvain, p. 26 (center left); © Leroy Simon/Visuals Unlimited, p. 26 (center right); Dave Monteith/Travel Arctic, GNWT, p. 29 (left); © TRIP/N. Price, p. 29 (right); City of Moncton, p. 30; Canadian Olympic Association/Mike Ridewood, p. 31 (bottom); Festival Acadien, Inc., p. 36 (left); © Roman Borgerding, p. 38 (left); Stratford Festival/David Cooper, p. 43 (left); Courtesy of Troubadour Records, p. 43 (center); Reuters/Fred Prouser/Archive Photos, p. 43 (right); © Diarama Stock Photos, Inc., p. 45. Cover photo of two girls on a boat, © Excel Images, Inc./Canadian Tourism Commission.

Copyright © 1999 by Carolrhoda Books, Inc.

All rights reserved. International copyright secured. No part of this book may be reproduced, stored in a retrieval system, or transmitted in any form or by any means—electronic, mechanical, photocopying, recording, or otherwise—without the prior written permission of Carolrhoda Books, Inc., except for the inclusion of brief quotations in an acknowledged review.

Carolrhoda Books, Inc.
c/o The Lerner Publishing Group
241 First Avenue North
Minneapolis, Minnesota 55401 U.S.A.

Website address: www.lernerbooks.com

Library of Congress Cataloging-in-Publication

Hamilton, Janice
Canada / by Janice Hamilton
    p. cm. — (A ticket to)
  Includes index.
  Summary: Discusses the people, geography, religion, language, customs, lifestyle, and culture of Canada.
    ISBN 1-57505-133-8 (lib. bdg. : alk. paper)
    1. Canada—Juvenile literature. I. Title. II. Title: Canada.
F1008.2.H26 1999
971—DC21   98-23114

Manufactured in the United States of America
1 2 3 4 5 6 – JR – 04 03 02 01 00 99

Contents

Welcome!	4	School Time	28
From the East	6	Sports	30
To the West	8	Religions	32
Lots of Water	10	Holidays	34
Weather	12	Festivals	36
Visitors to Stay	14	Art	38
First Canadians	16	Story Time	40
Busy Cities	18	Sing a Song	42
Two Languages	20	*New Words to Learn*	*44*
Getting Around	22	*New Words to Say*	*46*
Family	24	*More Books to Read*	*47*
What Is Cooking?	26	*New Words to Find*	*48*

Welcome!

Canada is a huge country on the **continent** of North America. Take a look at the map. Can you name the two things that touch Canada? If you guessed water and the United States, you are right. The Atlantic Ocean splashes Canada's

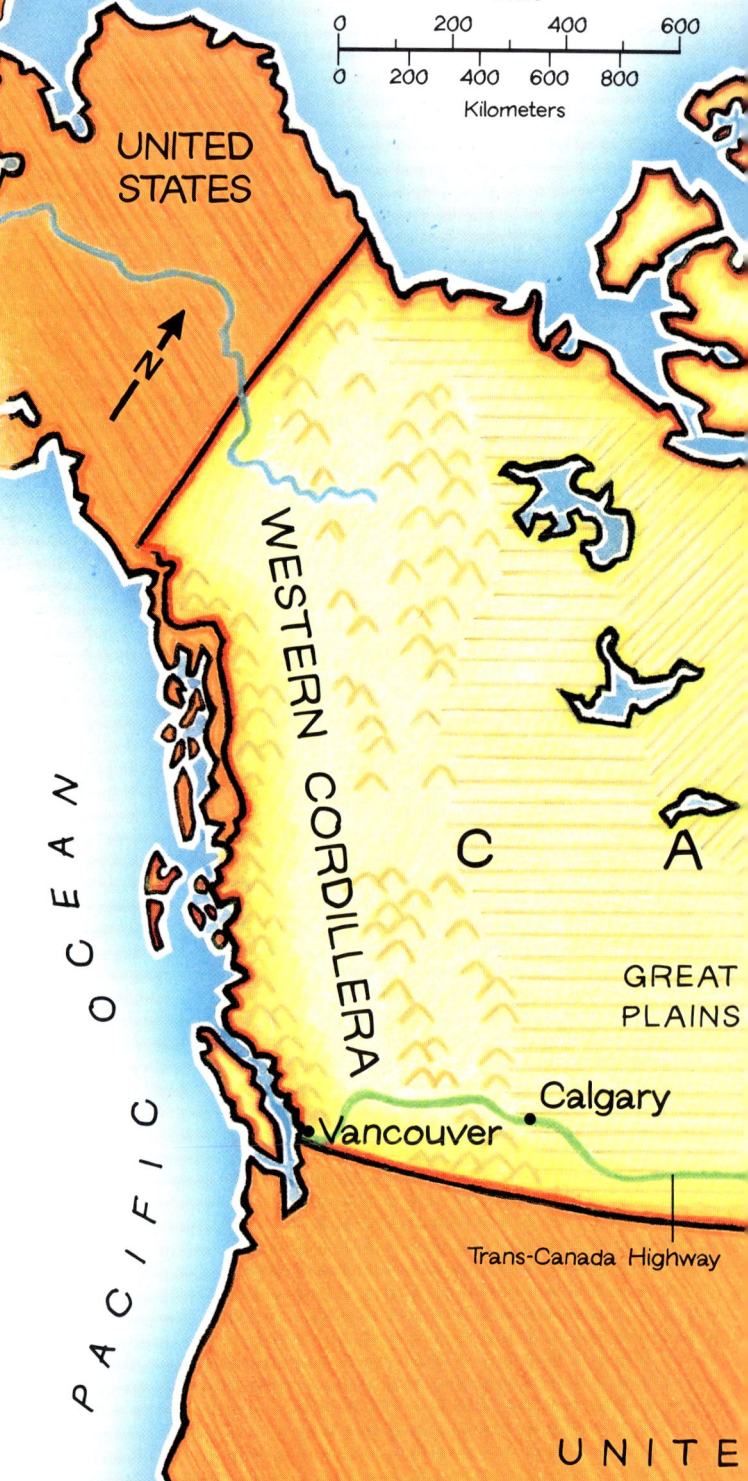

eastern side. The chilly Arctic Ocean lies to the north. The Pacific Ocean washes against Canada's western shore. And the United States meets Canada in the south and in the northwest.

5

From the East

Fishing villages dot Canada's eastern coast where small numbers of people live. But more Canadians live in the southeastern **lowlands** than anywhere else. Lowland farmers grow fruits and vegetables and raise chickens and cows.

Much of Canada's land is on the Canadian Shield.

Tons of fish swim in the waters off of Canada's coastline. It is the longest in the world!

The land is rocky and sort of flat with lots of lakes, streams, and swamps. Many dinosaur bones have been found here!

At open-air markets, farmers sell the fruits and vegetables that they grow in Canada's lowlands.

In and Out

At **high tide,** only trees show above the water at Flowerpot Rocks. At **low tide,** when the water washes out to sea, the rocks shaped like flowerpots appear!

Mountains, mountains, and more mountains. That is what you will find in western Canada.

To the West

Moving west from the Canadian Shield, the flat, rocky land gives way to the Great **Plains.** Cows love it here! They have lots of space to roam and plenty of grass to eat. If you keep going west, the land buckles up, and you can see the giant peaks of the Western Cordillera, a large **mountain range.** Do not go too far west. You will end up in the Pacific Ocean!

Map Whiz Quiz

Trace the outline of the map on pages four and five. In the Atlantic Ocean, put an E for east. Write an S for south in the United States. The W for west goes in the Pacific Ocean. At the squiggly top, put an N for north. Pick out two colors—one for the United States and one for all the water around Canada.

You can see for miles around on the flat Great Plains. Much of the country's grain (top) *and beef from cattle* (left) *comes from this area.*

Lots of Water

Come on in! The water is great!

If you were to try to count all of the lakes in Canada, you would be at it for a long time. But if you guessed two million, you would be pretty close. Some lakes are very small. Others are the perfect size for fishing and swimming. And five—called the Great Lakes—are so huge you cannot see the other side. See if you can remember their names. They are

Lakes Superior, Huron, Erie, Ontario, and Michigan. Canada and the United States share the Great Lakes—except for Lake Michigan, which sits only in the United States.

The St. Lawrence River links the Great Lakes with the Atlantic Ocean.

Way Deep!

In area, Lake Superior is the largest freshwater lake in the entire world! It is also the deepest of the Great Lakes. It is so deep that only parts of Lake Superior freeze completely.

Weather

Brrr! Canadians bundle up in winter. Temperatures in many places can dip low. Winter brings ice and snow. It is a good thing most Canadian kids like to skate and sled.

Because Canada is so far north, summers are short. But they are usually warm and sunny. Most summer days are perfect for a hike in the mountains or for fishing and diving from a dock.

Only strong plants can grow in the frozen north.

What could be more fun than sledding on a winter day? Hot chocolate anyone?

Slow Movers

In northern Canada, you will see lots of glaciers. Glaciers are huge sheets of ice that formed because ice and snow piled up for thousands of years. Every time snow does not melt after a storm, more layers of ice build up. The great glaciers creep along as they thaw and freeze every season.

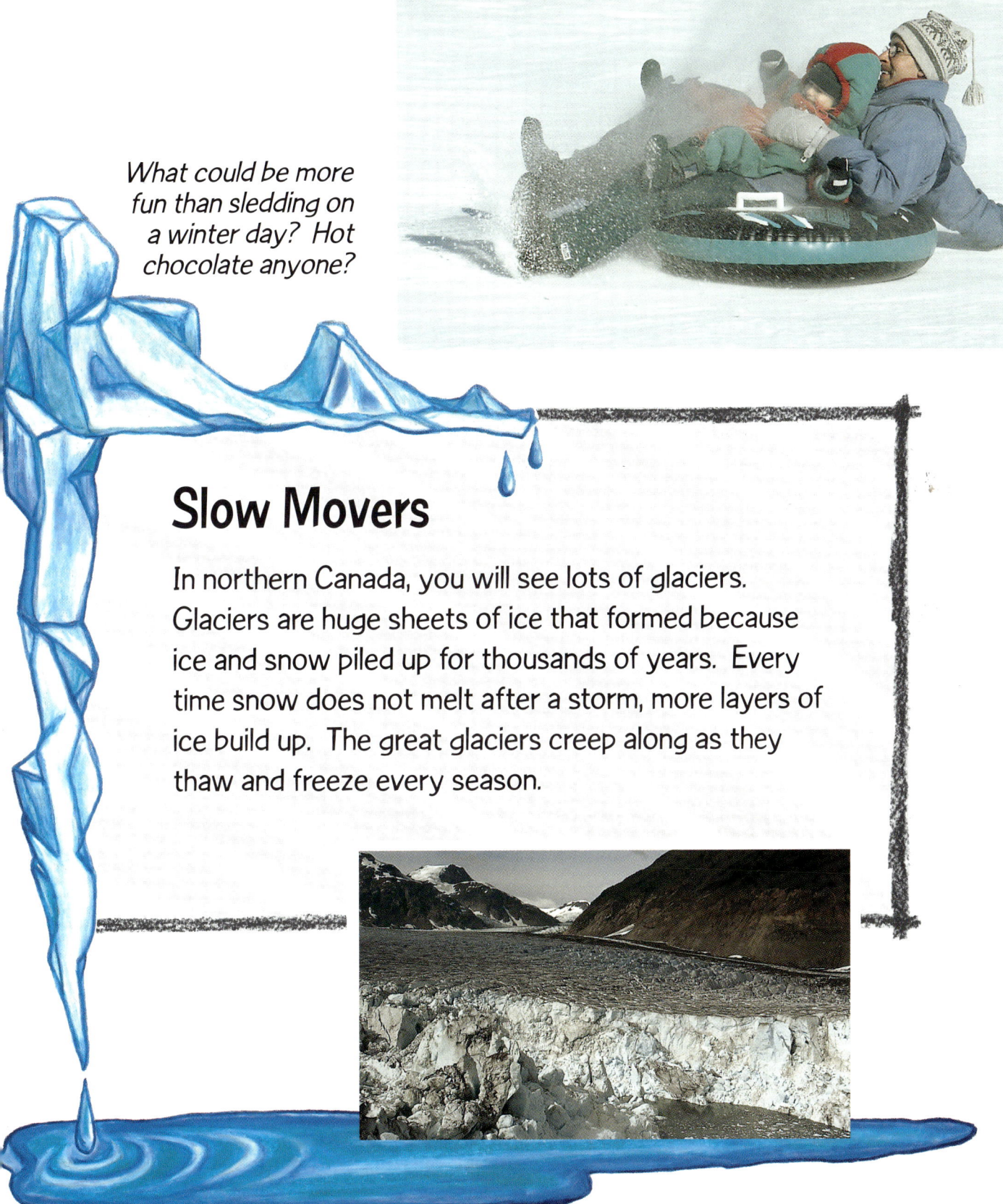

Canada has lots of different faces.

Visitors to Stay

Explorers from Europe landed long ago on Canada's shores. Soon they were followed by French and British settlers who came to find good fishing and hunting. These days the French and British make up Canada's two biggest **ethnic groups.** Much later people came from China, Italy, Poland, Jamaica, and Vietnam to make new homes in Canada.

Canadians of different ethnic groups share their food. Special cheeses (left) *come from Finland and Germany. Or grab a bite in Chinatown* (below).

Modern-day Indians carry on the traditions of their early relatives. During special holidays, they dance the same dances and wear traditional clothing as in the old days.

First Canadians

Canada's first people did not come by ship. They walked! A strip of land used to stretch from the continent of Asia to North America. Millions of years ago, people used this strip as a land bridge to cross into Canada. They hunted, fished, and collected fruits. In the

Inuit children (above) bundle up to stay warm. A woman uses a sewing machine (right) to patch her family's tent.

south, they lived in houses made of tree bark or animal skins. In the north, people built houses of snow, called **igloos.** Indians and Inuits are the modern-day relatives of the earliest Canadians.

Visitors find lots to do in Toronto. They can see a play or check out a cool museum.

Busy Cities

Most Canadians live in one of three big cities. Toronto is a very busy city on the edge of Lake

Dear Aunt Alice,

Today we skated on the world's longest skating rink. (I fell only a couple of times!) The skating rink is actually the Rideau Canal in Ottawa. A canal is sort of like a fake river. Rideau Canal is five miles long, so we did not skate the whole thing.

They are celebrating Winterlude here. We watched the ice-sculpting contest and the dogsled races. Mom says be sure to wear my hat.

See you soon!

Mike

Ride 'Em and Rope 'Em!

Every July in Calgary, **rodeo** lovers gather to watch the Calgary Exhibition and Stampede. Bull riders see how long they can hang on. Many people have cookouts and watch fireworks at night.

Ontario. Montreal, in the east, was built around a mountain on an island. Vancouver is right next to the Pacific Ocean. People go downtown to swim or to picnic while watching the big ships sail past.

In Vancouver, you could take a taxi to the beach!

This sign says, "beware" in two languages.

Two Languages

What's for breakfast? Capitaine Crounche (Captain Crunch)! Cereal boxes in Canada are printed with both French and English words. That is because Canadians speak two **national languages.** Most people in Canada speak English. But people in the **province** of Quebec—as well as in other, smaller communities—speak and write in French. And almost all the kids in Quebec go to French *écoles*, or schools.

Quebec

People from Quebec are Canadians. But many of them would like to have their own country called—what else?—Quebec. Many Québecois (French for people from Quebec) are relatives of the first French settlers. Many Canadians from other parts of Canada are relatives of the first English settlers. The Québecois do not want to lose their ties to French culture and language.

Try to figure out what this says in French. Bet you can!

Roads are scarce in northern Canada. To get there, visitors can take special planes that land on water. Splash!

Getting Around

Canadians love to drive. But with all that water in Canada, they sometimes need to take boats. A ferry is a flat boat that carries cars and people across water. Some ferry rides are short. Other trips are six hours long. You can eat lunch, read a book, and take a nap!

From Here to There

One way to travel Canada from coast to coast is by the Trans-Canada Highway. This 5,000-mile-long road goes over and under rivers and lakes. Cars cross bridges and go through tunnels to get across water. Once in a while, travelers get to take a ferry to reach the other side.

Moving along! Trains may not be the fastest way to travel. But passengers get a great look at Canada's countryside.

Family

Some Canadian kids do not have brothers or sisters. Lots of families live in cities.

But others have homes in the country, where kids have plenty of room to play.

Whether they fly kites (above) or hike in the mountains (left), Canadian families find time to have fun.

All in the Family

Here are the French words for some family members. Try them out on your own family.

grandfather	*grandpapa*	(grahn-pah-PAH)
grandmother	*grandmaman*	(grahn-mah-MAHN)
father	*papa*	(pah-PAH)
mother	*maman*	(mah-MAHN)
uncle	*oncle*	(OHN-kluh)
aunt	*tante*	(TAHNT)
son	*fils*	(FEES)
daughter	*fille*	(FEE)
brother	*frère*	(FREHR)
sister	*soeur*	(SUR)

Maple syrup (above) comes from the sap of a maple tree (inset).

Fiddleheads grow in the forest (above). They taste a little like spinach. Eat up!

What Is Cooking?

Some Canadian food may sound strange. They eat the tender shoots of ferns, called fiddleheads. Caribou meat (from a large deer) and arctic char (a fish) are some foods on a Canadian menu.

French Toast

Pure maple syrup is best served over a plate of hot French toast. Ask an adult to make you this meal some Saturday morning.

What you need:

2 eggs
1/4 cup milk
4 slices of bread
maple syrup

What to do:

Break the eggs into a dish with a wide bottom. Beat the eggs with a fork. Add the milk and beat some more.

Heat a pan over medium heat. Melt butter or margarine in the pan. Set a slice of bread in the egg mixture. Turn it over so both sides soak up the batter. Put soaked bread in pan and cook until it turns golden brown. Turn it over and cook the other side. Repeat with other slices, adding butter or margarine to the pan as needed. Serve with maple syrup. Mmm, mmm, good!

An outdoor classroom—what fun! These kids learn how parks can help protect plants and animals.

School Time

Canadian children start school when they are five years old. They learn reading, writing, math, social studies, and science. Some kids stay after school for fun activities such as ballet or arts and crafts. Most kids go to free public schools. But parents may pay to send their children to private schools that offer special programs. Either way, kids have homework.

You could ski or snowshoe to school if you lived here (below).

Inuit kids can go to schools where everything is taught in the Inuit language.

Sports

She shoots! She scores! Canadians are crazy about hockey. Kids play whenever they can. They shoot the puck after school and on weekends. Indoor and outdoor rinks allow kids to play in any season. During winter Canadians ski and snowboard. Summer means swimming, hiking, camping, and biking.

Canadians love the three S's— swimming, soccer, and skiing!

Hockey is fun for people of all ages.

Curling

Curling became an official sport of the Winter Olympics in 1998. The object of curling is to slide a large, round stone across a narrow ice rink. The team that gets the stone closest to a circle at the end of the rink wins. Each player on the four-member team has a different job to help the stone get to the target.

Religions

When the French and the British came to Canada, they brought their own customs,

languages, and religions. Most Canadians are Roman Catholic or

Indians celebrate with food, song and dance, and colorful costumes.

Protestant—the main religions of France and Britain. But Canada has people who belong to other religions, too. The number of Muslims and Jews is growing. Canada's Indians and Inuits believe that all people, animals, and plants have spirits watching over them.

Churches of many shapes, sizes, and faiths decorate Canada's towns and cities.

Canada Day is a time for marching bands and waving flags.

Holidays

Canadians love holidays. Whoopee! One of the biggest national holidays is Canada Day (July 1). On that day, Canadians celebrate their country's decision to make one nation out of many provinces.

On Canada Day, and most Canadian holidays, people enjoy picnics, parades, and fireworks.

Easter Eggs

Canadians whose relatives came from Ukraine (a country in eastern Europe) make beautiful Easter eggs, called *pysankas*. Each egg is carefully decorated. These colorful Easter eggs must be easy to find!

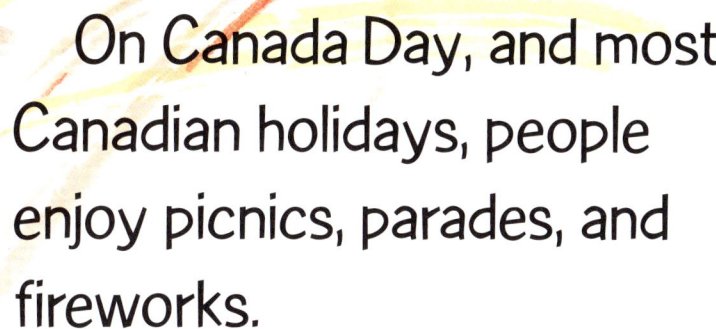

Relatives of the first French settlers celebrate the Acadian Festival with crazy costumes and parades (above). Bagpipe players (right) blow all day long during Gaelic Mod.

Festivals

Party down! Members of Canada's many ethnic groups celebrate their different cultures during festivals. The French Canadians of Quebec put together the

Hang on! A competitor in the pole-twisting contest balances as other players try to shake him off.

world's only French rodeo. During Gaelic Mod, Canada's Scottish people play music and have contests. The strange music of bagpipes drifts over the crowd. Meanwhile players compete to see who can throw a wooden pole the farthest. Canada's native peoples test their strength and skill during the Northern Games. They compete at drumming, pole twisting, and arm wrestling.

Art

Canada's scenery has moved many artists to draw and paint. But not all art is on a canvas. Many years ago, Canada's Inuit people carved tools and toys out of animal bones and animal horns. These days you can see them in museums.

The faces on these totem poles (above) *are not just playful and colorful. They tell stories about the families who made them.* (Left) *It is hard to believe that this cute carved owlet was once just a lump of soapstone.*

Modern-day Inuit artists carve figures of animals and people out of a soft rock called soapstone.

Totem Poles

Canada's native peoples are famous for their totem poles. Folks usually carve animal faces—one on top of another—into logs. Each family has its own pole. Native peoples assigned meanings to certain animals. So people can "read" another family's pole. What animals would your family's totem pole have?

Story Time

Kids laugh out loud when they read Canadian author, Robert Munsch's book, *I Have to Go!* It is a funny story about a little boy who remembers to *go* to the bathroom *after* he puts on his snowsuit.

Another Canadian writer, Paulette Bourgeois, spins tales about Franklin the turtle. He helps kids learn how to share and how to be brave in the dark.

You can read about this house and the feisty girl who lived there in Anne of Green Gables.

Telling Stories

A great many years ago—before stories were written down—native peoples said the stories out loud to one another. Grandparents told them to their grandchildren. Here is one they might have told while sitting around the fire at night. It is one of the many stories of how the world began.

In the beginning, there were no people. Only one piece of land existed, and Sea Lion owned it. The rest of the world was water. Crow stole Sea Lion's baby. Crow would not give the baby back until Sea Lion gave him some sand. Crow sprinkled the sand over the water to create the world. But Crow was lonely. So he carved Man and Woman from a tree and gave them life.

Sing a Song

Get ready for a toe-tapping good time with this Canadian fiddler.

It is hard not to tap your toes when Raffi plays his guitar and sings. Many kids know all the words to "Big Beautiful Planet" and "Frère Jacques." Can you sing along?

Canadians like moving to the beat. They dance to country, folk, and rock-and-roll. If their legs get tired, Canadians sit down and listen to the **symphony** or enjoy an **opera.**

Row, Row, Row

Have you ever sung songs to make a car trip seem shorter? When the French first came to Canada, they traveled long distances by canoe. To help them keep rowing, they sang song after song—loudly!

Actors (left), *songwriter Raffi* (above), *and rock-star Alanis Morisette* (right) *entertain Canadians of all ages.*

New Words to Learn

continent: Any one of seven large areas of land. The continents are Africa, Antarctica, Asia, Australia, Europe, North America, and South America.

ethnic group: A group of people with many things in common, such as language, religion, and customs.

high tide: The highest point reached when the water surface rises. **Low tide** is the lowest point. All bodies of water connected to the ocean rise and fall twice a day.

igloo: A shelter made from blocks of ice, wood, or stone.

lowland: Flat land that is lower than the surrounding area.

mountain range: A series, or group, of mountains—the parts of the earth's surface that rise high into the sky.

A bighorn sheep climbs a steep mountainside.

national language: The language spoken by most people of a country. It is the language of government and is spoken in most schools and businesses.

opera: A play in which the actors sing instead of speak their parts.

plain: A large area of flat land.

Summer fun!

province: A region within a country. Like a state, it can make decisions for some types of activities, but must follow laws that apply to the whole country.

rodeo: A contest usually performed on horseback. Rodeo events include roping calves and riding bulls.

symphony: A musical concert. Symphony musicians often play stringed instruments (like violin and piano), winds (like flute and clarinet), and percussion (like drums).

New Words to Say

Capitaine Crounche	KAH-PEE-ten CROHNSH
caribou	CAIR-ih-boo
cordillera	kohr-duh-LAIR-uh
écoles	AY-kohl
Frére Jacques	FREHR-uh ZHAH-kuh
Gaelic Mod	GAY-lihk MAHD
glacier	GLAY-shur
Huron	HYOO-rahn
Inuit	IH-noo-wuht
Michigan	MIH-shih-gehn
Montreal	mahn-tree-AWL
Ontario	ahn-TEH-ree-oh
Ottawa	AH-tuh-wah
Paulette Bourgeois	pawl-EHT BOOR-zhwah
pysanka	py-SAHN-kuh
Quebec	kwih-BEHK
Québecois	kay-behk-KWAHZ
Rideau Canal	rih-DOH kuh-NAL
Toronto	toh-ROHN-toh
Ukraine	YOO-krayn
Vancouver	van-KOO-vur

More Books to Read

Barbeau, Marius. *The Golden Phoenix and Other French-Canadian Fairy Tales.* New York: Walck, 1958.

Bourgeois, Paulette. *Franklin and the Tooth Fairy.* New York: Scholastic, 1996.

Bourgeois, Paulette. *Franklin's Blanket.* New York: Scholastic, 1996.

Burns, Diane. *Sugaring Season: Making Maple Syrup.* Minneapolis: Carolrhoda Books, Inc., 1990.

Haskins, Jim. *Count Your Way through Canada.* Minneapolis: Carolrhoda Books, Inc., 1989.

Jensen, Julie. *Beginning Hockey.* Minneapolis: Lerner Publications Company, 1996.

Lye, Keith. *Take a Trip to Canada.* London: Franklin Watts, 1983.

Munsch, Robert. *I Have to Go!* Toronto, Ontario: Annick Press, Ltd., 1987.

Temko, Florence. *Traditional Crafts from Native North America.* Minneapolis: Lerner Publications Company, 1997.

New Words to Find

art, 38–39

cities, 18–19, 24

ethnic groups, 15, 36
explorers, 14–15, 21

families, 24–25
farmers, 6, 9
festivals, 36–37
fishing, 6, 10
Flowerpot Rocks, 7
food, 15, 26–27

glaciers, 13

hockey, 30
holidays, 34–35
houses, 17, 24

Inuit and Indians, 17, 33, 37, 38–39, 41

lakes, 7, 10–11, 19
languages, 20–21, 25

map of Canada, 4–5
mountains, 9, 19
music, 42–43

oceans, 4–5, 9, 19

people, 14–15, 16–17

religions, 32–33

schools, 20, 28–29
sports, 10, 12, 19, 30–31
stories, 40–41

totem poles, 39
Trans-Canada Highway, 23
travel methods, 22–23

weather, 12–13